D1294193

The Twelve of Hats Christmas

Written by:
Brett O. Parson

Illustrated by:
Holly Parson Nielsen

Book Design by:
Justin Parson
whatimagination.com

Published by:

PARSON PUBLISHING
www.parsonpublishing.com

To my wife Heidi who really wrote the book and let me put my name on it.

- BOP

To my crazy fun Big Brothers!

- HPN

Here we meet
Thaddeus Willard Elf,
which is a bit hard to say,

So his friends call him T.W.
as they pass him by each day.

T.W. was a Hat Elf
who took pride in his trade.

He worked with such care
on each hat that he made.

Hat Elves are among the most creative of minds,
And T.W. could make hats of all shapes and all kinds:

Large and small, short and tall,
Some are knitted and others are fitted.
Some have lights that warm and glow,
While others are bright and white as the snow.

Though his favorite of all wasn't shiny or tall.
It wasn't as **clean**

or as **bright**

or as **new**,

And right on the front
was stitched **T.W.**

T'was a day toward the end of the month of December,
When a letter arrived with a date to remember!

You're invited!

Santa

Santa was having a
BIG WINTER'S BALL.
With Hat Elves
and Shop Elves
and presents
And ALL!

What you might not know is on each Christmas Eve,
It's Santa's birthday, is that hard to believe?

T.W. wanted to give Santa a gift full of joy,
But what could he bring? Candy? Clothing? a Toy?

Well, he's a Hat Elf, of course,
so he knew what to bring

Better than racecars or baseballs
or green silly string!

A Hat! A Hat! His Very Best Hat!

But which one . . .

which one . . .

. . . which one would be that?

He thought of it long, then he thought of it quick,
And decided to bring them ALL for Saint Nick!

He went through his shop
and picked hats he loved most,

Then sipped up some cocoa
and ate all his toast.

He placed eleven hats
all snug in his pack,

Threw them over his shoulder
and onto his back.

On his way to St. Nick's,
he saw in the snow,

A man with a scarf
'neath the sun's golden glow.

Yet, the snowman looked cold with his head round and bare,
So T.W. lent him a hat - at least one he could spare.

"If I give him just ONE,

I'll still have TEN more,

And these hats are for giving,

that's just what they're for!"

As he journeyed along, he had a surprise,

The scariest thing he had seen with two eyes!

A reindeer in the river was splashing about,

He'd broken through the ice and he **couldn't get out!**

Quick as a flash to his backpack he flew,

Searching his hats for one sturdy and true!

He threw out the hat across ice and the snow,

And pulled out his friend with a hefty heave-ho!

Just as T.W. came into town,
his triumphant smile
turned into a frown.

The streetlight was broken,
the traffic insane,

Backed up for miles
on Candy Cane Lane!

There were elves in sleighs
and critters to spare:

Reindeer and birds and
a white polar bear!

Why of all days was the traffic like this?
If it didn't clear fast, Santa's party he'd miss!

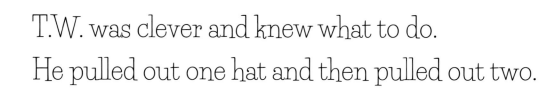

T.W. was clever and knew what to do.
He pulled out one hat and then pulled out two.

One hat was red, one yellow, one green!
These were the brightest hats you've ever seen!

The hats were perfect - beaming so bright.
Bursting with color! Wow! What a sight!

Those hats did the trick -
they moved traffic through town.
'Til the street became empty
with no one around!

EXCEPT - for a long line
of bustling elves.
Who came for the cupcakes
and cookies on shelves!

The bakery was **packed tight** with all the right stuffins,

And sugary sweet things
right down to the muffins.

Gingerbread men
made of sugar and spice,

With buttercream frosting
that looked just like ice.

Dishes and bowls
piled as high as a tree!

All had been used, which left
none that were free!

At last, with one batch of
sweet cupcakes to bake,

No mixing bowl found
that could mix up the cake!

Slick as ice skates T.W. flew! He opened his pack - he knew what to do!

He pulled out a round-shaped hat from his bag,
One he kept clean and new with its tag.

"This bowler could work as a bowl for the mix,
To stir in the chocolate and peppermint sticks."

Soon all was finished
and sure to delight,   And EVERY last cupcake was sold out that night!

Then the clock sounded, it now was past eight.
So much to stop him and make him quite late!

He burst through the door and onto the street
As fast as he could with his tiny elf feet!

As he hurried along past a house made of stone,
Four children cried out in a whimpering moan.

Their stockings *unraveled* in heaps on the floor,

Once hung on the mantle, but not anymore!

They were chewed up and scattered by a small Christmas mouse,
That snuck through the door and right into the house.

The children grew tired and needed to sleep,
So they went to their beds with not even a peep.

T.W. tip-toed
 to the fireplace mantle,

Guided alone by a
pine-scented candle.

He hung the four hats in a row
ONE-BY-ONE

And set them just right
'til the last one was done.

But, as he quietly crept outside the window,

His hat became l o o s e

and fell in the snow.

Just then he felt
a cold breeze on his head,

No trace of his hat -
not even a thread!

He searched and he searched across meadows of frost,

But sadly his favorite old hat had been lost!

No time left for sorrow, the Ball would start soon!
Heart-broken he pushed on underneath the full moon . . .

At last to Santa's shop
he timidly stepped,
Thankful
to know
that
ONE HAT
he
had
kept.

But just when he placed his elf foot on the stair,
He heard a soft "chirp" fade away in the air.

He looked to the spot where he heard the faint sound,
And saw a small bird huddled cold on the ground.

This bird, he could see,
was chilled to the beak

By the cold winter's night
that was **frozen** and **bleak.**

T.W. paused and struggled inside,

"Should I just walk by - and say that I tried?"

Well, his choice was simple - he'd proven his stuff.
He pulled out his **last hat** of feathery fluff,

Then scooped up the bird and snuggled it tight,

In a hat **full of love** on this

Christmas Eve night.

He knew he had nothing
for Santa's big day

Because he had given
his hats all away.

"And even what's more,"
he thought to himself,

"What will they think
of a poor hatless elf?"

Now, something that's known
throughout the North Pole:

An elf with no hat
looks rather quite droll.

After all, have **you** ever seen
an elf with no hat?

Especially in public . . .
imagine that!

He walked in the room,
with his head bald and bare,

To a crowd of elf faces
with open-eyed stare!

Just then, right behind him, someone cleared his throat.
He turned to find Santa in his red and white coat.

"I've watched as you've given your presents away
To all those in need, which made you delay.

A kind deed was shared
with each hat that you gave."

"And blessed others greatly
in ways smart and brave."

Santa opened his sack,
and with gentle expression

Looked down at the elf
with the kindest compassion.

"You know it's my birthday -
of course this is true,

Yet I spend my time
giving to people like you."

"I do this on purpose

because I believe,

It's really

much better to give

than receive."

As the crowd departed and went on their way,
T.W. paused - he wanted to stay.

He walked to the hearth, near fire's warm glow,
And looked at his gift tied up with a bow.

He opened the lid as he quietly sat

And found in the box
lay his favorite old hat.

It wasn't as **clean**

or as **bright**

or as **new,**

And right on the front
was stitched **T.W.**

He made up his mind
right then and right there,

To always help others
and serve them with care.

And now he invites **YOU**
to do as he's done:

Give deeds of true kindness
to bless **EVERYONE!**